THE 90-SECOND LIFE COACH

HOW TO REALISE AND LIVE THE LIFE OF YOUR DREAMS

FARHAN QURESHI

Published by Digitopia Studios Ltd. 2017

Copyright © Farhan Qureshi 2017

ISBN 978-0-9927340-4-6

Farhan Qureshi has asserted his right under the Copyright, Designs and Patent Act 1988 to be identified as the author of this work.

This book is sold subject to the condition that it shall not, by the way of trade or otherwise, be lent, resold, hired out or reproduced in any part or by any means or otherwise circulated without the author's prior consent in any form of binding or cover other than that in which it is published and without a similar condition, including this condition, being imposed on the subsequent purchaser.

Disclaimer: This book contains information from many years of research and practical experience. Whilst this has been successful for the author, no guarantees are made that the same results will apply to the reader. Advice and knowledge in here must be tailored to the reader's individual circumstances.

Written by Farhan Qureshi www.workingParent.info
Edited by Mintoi Chessa-Florea www.theenergyspace.com
and Vicki Watson www.callistogreen.com
Cover Design by Farhan Qureshi
Book Layout and Design by Vicki Watson

About the Author

Farhan is a filmmaker and blogger from London, in the UK. Having spent ten years working as a CGI and VFX artist, Farhan has worked on some of the biggest Hollywood movies including three Harry Potter movies, Batman, Alien, Predator and
Pirates, as well as working as a lead artist at the London Olympic 2012 ceremonies. Farhan is now a leader in the digital space, designing and developing next-generation digital products and solutions.

Several years ago Farhan took a keen interest in the area of self-help and motivation. Having been a student of this subject, Farhan has studied all the great motivational experts, and having met and spent time with them, Farhan has applied these lessons to his own life, living many of his ambitions to become a professional filmmaker, four-time Amazon bestselling author, successful blogger and YouTuber.

Farhan is really passionate about helping people. His previous books include VFX and CG Survival Guide for Producers and Filmmakers, which helps independent filmmakers and producers effectively prepare and put VFX/CG into their movies.

Farhan believes that dads are really important, not only in bringing up well-rounded children but in having a wider responsibility in society. His next book, Working Dad, was a self-help book aimed at fathers who struggle with trying to balance their careers with family life.

Farhan then went onto write the amazingly successful Web Analytics for Bloggers book, helping independent and start-up bloggers to quickly implement and analyse Google Analytics into their blogs and help them find their audience.

To visit Farhan's blogs, go to www.digitopiafilm.com, www.workingparent.info and www.digitopiadigital.com. Find Farhan on IMDB here www.imdb.com/name/nm1629604 and on Amazon at www.amazon.co.uk/Farhan-Qureshi/e/B00J7AT56Y.

About the Editor

Mintoi has worked as a financial healthcare journalist for nearly ten years writing about pharma, biotech and medtech stocks and startups. Alongside this role she became a Training Editor, implementing a mentoring scheme for new starters in the editorial teams.

Mintoi is passionate about people's self development, both as a journalist or as someone seeking to learn techniques to perform better at work or feel more fulfilled in life.

She is a keen reader of the new science and quantum theory and its impact on medicine, therapeutics and everyday living.

About the Editor/Layout Designer

Vicki Watson is a writer, editor, book designer and publisher, whose publications have ranged from business books and teacher resource guides to children's workbooks, drama, fiction and poetry. After a career as a teacher and deputy headteacher, she decided to focus on her love of language  and design and set up Callisto Green, a vibrant and dynamic writing and design venture and publishing imprint, where she now spends her days playing with words and pictures.

When she's not scribbling in her notebook, her many interests include playing the clarinet, rock-climbing, stargazing and playing chess. She lives in Wiltshire with her husband and three sons.

Vicki can be contacted by emailing vicki@callistogreen.com or through her website at www.callistogreen.com.

Contents

Introduction 1

PART ONE:
YOUR MINDSET 7

    Chapter 1: You have total control over yourself 9

    Chapter 2: Why having more stuff won't make you happier 11

    Chapter 3: Daydream – a lot 15

    Chapter 4: Everyone has fear 17

    Chapter 5: Fixed or growth mindset 21

    Chapter 6: Stop thinking life would have been better with someone else 25

    Chapter 7: Be what you want to be; don't wait for permission 29

    Chapter 8: The power of saying sorry 31

    Chapter 9: We all make mistakes in life, so cut yourself some slack 35

PART TWO: YOUR ACTIVITIES 39

    Chapter 10: Reclaim your life, your 'To Be' list 41

    Chapter 11: What are you waiting for? Do it now! 45

    Chapter 12: Urgent versus important activities – how to manage your day 47

    Chapter 13: Drink more water, get more sleep 53

    Chapter 14: Would you rather have pain or regret? 57

    Chapter 15: Choose how you spend your 'own' time 61

Chapter 16: Control – where are you placing your focus? 65

PART THREE: HARNESSING THE WORLD AROUND YOU 69

Chapter 17: The secret of win-win: seek first to understand 71

Chapter 18: Why you shouldn't compare yourself to others and how to stop doing it 75

Chapter 19: Choose your friends carefully 79

Chapter 20: What if you don't have anyone to support you? 81

Chapter 21: Stop trying to be right all the time 85

Chapter 22: Everything happens for a reason 89

Chapter 23: Talk ideas, not people 93

Chapter 24: You catch more bees with honey than with vinegar 97

Chapter 25: Talk to those who've been there 101

PART FOUR: MAKING IT REAL 105

Chapter 26: Create a vision board 107

Chapter 27: So what if it's difficult? Do it anyway! 111

Chapter 28: Step outside the complacent zone 115

Chapter 29: You don't need anyone's approval 119

Chapter 30: How to use the Pareto 80:20 rule in your favour 123

Chapter 31: Discernment and when to say 'No' 127

Chapter 32: Accept your weaknesses, focus on your strengths 131

Chapter 33: Always continue to move forwards 135

Ciao Ciao 137

x

Introduction

Hi there. First of all thanks for picking up this book. I'll spare you the normal long openings to a book with pages of introductions and get straight to the point. I want to help you improve your life. In fact, I want to give you a no-nonsense guide to improving your life and achieving your dreams in 90 seconds a day.

So first of all, who am I and why should you be listening to me?

You're busy, insanely busy. There are things you want to accomplish in life, burning ambitions that you never seem to have time to accomplish, and the dreams that you once had now seem to be getting further and further away as you become entrenched in the demands of modern-day life.

No matter how hard you work, you never seem to get to where you want to be.

No matter how motivated you get, you don't actually progress forwards.

Motivation is great. It gets you all excited and you feel brilliant. For a while, you go off into a sprint, but soon it feels as though you're running through thick goo and in no particular direction. No matter how fired up you are, if you don't know in which direction you're heading, then you're going to get lost or stuck very quickly.

Or worse, perhaps your life is drifting in the wrong direction, and the more you try to steer yourself back, the further adrift you become. You feel as if you're helpless and have little to no control over your life. In short, your life is not quite how you had once imagined it would be.

Right?

Fear not, dear friend. My life was like that too for a long period of time. But then I started taking a real interest into personal development, self-help, 'The Secret' and the law of attraction – which goes way beyond motivation. I managed to train myself up in the principles and techniques that I learnt from many masters. I've managed to change my life from one where I was totally controlled by circumstances and controlled by what others wanted, to a life where I pick and choose what I want to do and live life on my own terms.

Up to 2014 I had a really well-paid job doing CGI and VFX. In 2014 the bottom fell out of the UK CGI and VFX market and I totally crashed. I had to completely re-invent myself and start my career again from the ground up in a brand new field. Within sixteen months I had managed to get myself a 300% pay rise, doing fewer hours and having more spare time than at any other point in my career.

I now have the freedom and flexibility to do what I want. I spend my time writing books, making movies, blogging and doing cool digital projects, whilst being able to spend more time with my kids doing really fun things. Best of all, work doesn't get in the way of my lifestyle.

Why you should be reading this book?

Genuinely, I recognise the pain you're going through. I've been there, and I wanted to write this book to help you. Using the techniques and lessons that I've learnt, I managed to turn my situation around in under two years. I wanted to write a concise and 'to the point' book so that you can live a better life, a life you want to live, rather than a life that's imposed upon you or one that you feel obliged to live.

There are a lot of books out there that cover the same material as this one. But what I've done here is to structure the book in a concise way that gets straight to the heart of the matter; each chapter should take roughly 90 seconds to read.

Why 90 seconds, though?

I've been on long and expensive training courses and while these courses are great, they're not accessible to everyone. Maybe people don't have time to give up a whole week. Oftentimes the courses are pretty expensive and therefore preclude those people who need the help the most.

I've chosen 90 seconds because everyone has 90 seconds to spare a day. If someone won't or can't spare 90 seconds a day, then they're really not serious about improving their life.

Can you really change your life in 90 seconds a day?

Absolutely!

What I've done is to take the very essence of the life lessons that I've learnt and experienced, and crystallised it here for you to take away in a series of 90-second short chapters.

Of course some people are going to say that this is impossible, that it simply can't be done in 90 seconds, that the title of this book is a shameless marketing gimmick designed to sell books.

You're thinking that too, right?

Well, here's the proposition. Given the hectic nature of your life right now, you may not have weeks or thousands of dollars/pounds/euros/insert your currency here to invest in a week-long retreat.

So take my solution, 90 seconds a day and a 'ridiculously' low purchase price (at about 1% of the cost of taking a full-blown course). By the time you finish each chapter (90 seconds, as you've gathered) you will be so much more empowered to be able to change your life, knowing exactly what needs to be done, how and most importantly why. In fact, this introduction is the longest chapter in the whole book.

What will you get out of this book?

We're about to embark on a journey, a special journey, a journey with the most important person in the world. It's a journey with yourself.

Through each chapter you will get to know yourself better. And by the time you finish the book, you will have learnt :

- how your mind and thoughts shape your reality
- how to bring about change in your life
- how to create your own reality
- how the world operates and
- how you can use that operating model to your benefit

Not bad for a 90-second investment.

You could either read a chapter a day or the whole book in one go – it's entirely feasible. I've structured the book into four main parts where we focus on:

- your mindset
- your day-to-day activities
- dealing and making your way in the world

around you and

- how to make it real

Feel free to read them in order, to jump around a bit, or even jump completely randomly around the book – whichever way it works best for you.

Ready?

Let's go!

PART ONE: YOUR MINDSET

In this first part of the book, we are going to focus on the most powerful asset you have – your thoughts. We are going to learn how your mind can predetermine the outcomes that you're going to receive.

This is the logical starting point for everything.

Farhan Qureshi

Chapter 1: You have total control over yourself

Events that go on in the world can be broken down into two groups:

- things you can control and
- things you can't control

Things that fall into the second category include those relating to the world around you, for example, the weather, geo-politics, whether the train will be on time or whether there'll be a traffic jam when you're already late to work – you can't control any of this.

But you can control yourself!

Specifically, you can control your reactions to whatever the world, whatever life, throws at you.

So what does that mean?

It means you can either choose to let these things affect you and get you down or you can choose not to be affected by any of the things you can't control.

Either way, it's your choice.

You can choose to start swearing at the train driver as he shuts the doors three seconds before you got there, or you can choose to say, 'Okay, never mind, there'll be another one in a few minutes so I'll just chill out for a while.'

You can choose to get all defensive and tense when you see your boss ringing your phone or you can choose to say to her, 'Hey what's up? What can I help you with?'

While it can be difficult to control how you feel in any given situation, you do have total control over how you respond in any given situation – that's pretty powerful.

So here's what I want you to do. The next time something happens that you are dreading, make a choice. You can either choose to let the event get you down, get you stressed out and depressed, and allow it to eat away and ultimately destroy you, or you can choose to say, 'Oh well, never mind. These things happen. There was a valuable lesson in there for me – it made me stronger.'

Which choice do you think will improve your life?

Which choice is going to help you move forwards, feel happier, be more present, healthier, have a better life and achieve your dreams?

> No one can choose for you. This is one of those things over which you have 100% total control – and that's pretty awesome! Take back control over how you respond to events in your life.

Chapter 2: Why having more stuff won't make you happier

From the moment you were born, every single media and advertising outlet has been bombarding you with the message that you need more stuff to be happy. Whether it's a new phone (which is identical in almost every way to your current phone), a wristband that tells you your heart rate and temperature (because only a loser would actually wear a plain watch), the latest designer suit (with the label on the inside where no-one will ever see it anyway) or even worse, a designer bag (because you need to advertise their product for them), we have been programmed since birth that having 'things' will make us happier and somehow make us into better people!

So does having all this stuff actually make us any happier?

It probably made you feel good for a while to have that pair of designer sunglasses – it certainly felt great posting pictures on social media with your new wares – but how long did that feeling last? How often did you keep checking your status to see who'd 'liked' it? Did you get enough 'likes'? How long before you started wondering about all those who didn't 'like' or 'comment'? Did you focus more on those people than on those who took a single second to hit the 'like' button?

I learnt this lesson many years ago. Obviously looking and feeling particularly miserable one day, my friend asked me what was wrong. I said to him, 'It's because I don't have a girlfriend.' His reply was so profound that it changed my outlook immediately. He said, 'So what? You think having someone else will make you happy?'

What I took away from that (and I appreciate that he may have meant something else) was that nobody or nothing else can make you happy, until you are happy inside.

Happiness is already within you, it just needs unlocking. Happiness may not be those shiny 'things' that the media says you need to be happy, but by allowing yourself to be happy with who you are, you will grow and achieve what you want in life. And it won't be superficial, material things. It will be things like fulfilment, a sense of being, and the knowledge that you are accomplishing your goals. That's something a TV ad can't sell.

This change, coupled with the law of attraction, will bring more happiness into your life. For me, deciding that I would just be happy allowed a remarkable thing to happen almost immediately. By attracting into my life things that made me happy, I started doing all the things that I wanted to do and started to get more and more out of all the things that made me happy. It didn't have to do with anything material – I didn't even have a car at the time or much money – but it was the things that I was 'doing' that made me happy, not the 'having'.

In fact, when I was doing my master's at university, I remember living in a very modest house surrounded by great flatmates and loads of friends, having fun every day. I felt truly happy because I was doing exactly what I wanted to do with so many great people, having so much fun – yet I had no car, no fancy apartment and no flash watch (in fact no watch at all).

You see, the feeling leads to the action, and the action then leads to the result. Start with feeling happy with what you have. That way, you'll then start to do the things you want to do, and when you're grateful and happy, you won't spend your time whinging and bitching about how awful your life is. Instead, you'll see and appreciate all the great things about your life. As you might expect, the type of actions you'll take when you're in that space will result in you achieving the things that you want. You may not hit those results you want immediately, but think of this as a flow:

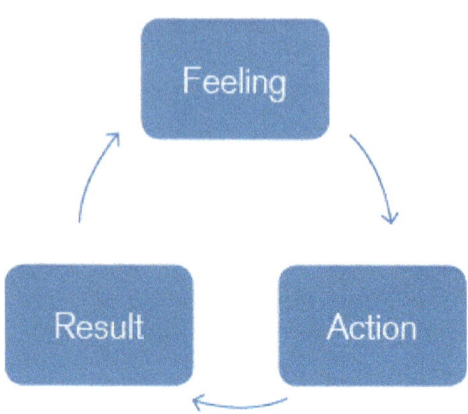

You'll certainly get closer to the results you want and feel better about life too.

> Happiness does not come from a place of 'having'; it comes from a place of 'being'. And the more you 'be' who you want to be, the happier and more fulfilled you will become.

Chapter 3: Daydream – a lot

Probably much like myself, you were told at school to 'pay attention' and 'stop daydreaming'. I've often wondered why daydreaming has earned such a bad reputation. Is it really something so negative?

As I progressed through my learning journey over the years, I found a new name for daydreaming; it's called 'imagineering' or 'visualising'.

I think not only is it healthy but it's in fact vital to explore your own imagination, where no one, no institution, no boss can tell you what you are allowed or not allowed to think – and just dream about what you want your life to be like.

It's here in your imagination (and your subconscious) where you can be completely free to think whatever you want to without anybody judging you or telling you 'no', or even worse, having to conform to what society expects you to be.

Once you can see in your imagination what you truly want, then you can start taking the steps to achieve it.

Essentially this means plotting out where you currently are, compared to where you want to be. We'll go into more detail in the later chapters about the tasks that you'll have to do and the obstacles that you'll have to overcome – Well you didn't expect it to be easy, did you? – but for now, daydream and daydream a lot. These are the images you will be following.

Without these images, you will start to conform to what society expects you to be. Do you want to live out society's expectations or do you want to attain your higher self and fulfil your own dreams?

Of course you understand the difference between 'daydreaming' and 'wishing your life away'. They are, after all, two completely different activities. 'Wishing your life away' is a waste of time and is about trying to escape your problems, whereas 'daydreaming' is about seeing what you want. The latter isn't about 'escaping', but allows you to explore and achieve.

And daydreaming isn't the end of the journey, but only the starting point, that place where you set your destination. Without this destination in mind, your life will be aimless wandering, going round in circles. With no goal in sight, you may work hard and put in a lot of effort, but ultimately you'll end up going nowhere. In the following chapters I'll give you the exact tools to get to that destination but for now, concentrate on the dreaming.

> Dream about where it is you want to get to, and the rest will fall into place.

Chapter 4: Everyone has fear

There are a lot of excuses that people give for not working towards their goal. Their excuses are wide and varied, including:

- their situation
- their upbringing
- their job
- the economy
- their partner/boss/parents/kids/in-laws

This list of excuses is endless, but here's the real truth: they're afraid and scared.

Of course, everyone is afraid. You haven't cornered the market on fear. Whether it's the fear of failure or fear of the sheer hard work involved, everyone's scared to a certain degree.

If the truth be told, I'm afraid of writing this book. After all, what will people say, and will they laugh at me if I don't sell any copies? But actually, those things are superficial fears, and there are two things that are far deeper than the fear of failure:

- we're afraid that we'll have to change and
- we're afraid that we might succeed

The first one is quite easy to understand. In order to accomplish the 'thing' that you want will require you to change, and no one likes change. The very mention of the word can make us uncomfortable, since we are creatures of habit and even though we understand its importance, change does not come naturally to the majority of us.

Change means we have to look ourselves in the mirror and face some uncomfortable truths about ourselves. Maybe we're lazy and we're afraid to make more effort, maybe we blame others and change would mean that we have to accept responsibility, or maybe we're with the wrong partner and change means that we have to be brave and tell them. Whatever it is that you're afraid of, you have to overcome it, because that thing that you're unwilling to change is holding you back from the true happiness that you crave.

The second deeper fear, the fear of success might sound a little crazy. But it's true nonetheless.

In order to succeed, you'll have to become the true person that you are capable of, that higher self. It means letting go of the person you are now and being mature enough to know there are no valid excuses.

It means being brave enough to accept that the only thing stopping yourself is you.

We're really not afraid of failure nearly as much as we are afraid of success because what happens next? If you succeed, what do you do after? Believe me, the thing that you want to succeed at today is merely a stepping stone to your next goal and next success – it's called growth and it's waiting for you once you overcome your initial fears.

Farhan Qureshi

Chapter 5: Fixed or growth mindset

The type of mindset you have will greatly affect what you can accomplish. Whether you see something as a 'problem' or an 'opportunity' will in turn colour your outlook on how you will enjoy or not enjoy your life. You can probably guess which one will give you a better life, so I'll get right into telling you how to shift from a fixed mindset into a growth mindset.

When something unexpected and undesirable happens, how do you see it?

Do you think, 'Oh no, I really don't need this right now! I have never even done this before. I don't know how to do it, and therefore I can't do it'?

Have a think about the last time you heard one of these statements said by someone you know. Whether they realise it or not, by reacting in this way they are operating from a fixed mindset. Are they an impressive person, have they accomplished anything, and do you want to be like that person?

Okay, now think about yourself. You have goals, ambitions and dreams to live. Chances are that the thing you want to do is going to require hard work, resilience and stretching yourself – if it didn't involve these things then it wouldn't be much of a goal.

Keep your dream in mind. Most likely it will make you excited and fill you with hope and energy. Just thinking about achieving it should give you intense satisfaction and happiness.

But there's that voice, the voice that says, 'Huh, who are you kidding? You can't do this! Who are you to think you can? There are too many things in your way, plus you don't even have a clue how to do it.'

Don't worry. You're not alone; we all hear some variant of that voice. The common mistake is listening to it. Most people pay attention to that negative, inner voice and reason to themselves, 'Yes, it's true, I don't know how to do this, I can't do this, who was I kidding to think I ever could?' and then they simply give up.

That is a fixed mindset and something that society has scripted us into from when we were young. When you said that you wanted to be a footballer and everyone laughed and told you that it was impossible or when everyone was waiting for you to fail so they could point out that 'you couldn't do it', fixed mindsets were at play. When all you ever hear is, 'No, you can't do it,' over time you start to believe what you're being told. It's a technique that was designed hundreds and hundreds of years ago to keep us in 'our place'.

However, things are only true if you want them to be true, and if you want to change from a fixed mindset to a growth mindset, then you can. In fact, it's as easy as reading this line to yourself:

> 'I can do it, because I can learn and adapt to achieve anything. I can. I will. I must.'

Suddenly that inner voice changes from, 'You can't do that,' to 'Okay, so what you need to do next is...' and the growth mindset starts to plot every task out. It's at this point that you realise there weren't even that many tasks in your way and they certainly weren't difficult. In fact, it's going to be great fun finding ways to navigate past them!

> Your life will start to improve from the very second you shift to a growth mindset. DO IT RIGHT NOW; it takes a single second.

Farhan Qureshi

Chapter 6: Stop thinking life would have been better with someone else

For those of us in a relationship, we all know that it can be a choppy ride. The easy temptation is to think that our lives would have been better with someone else, that somehow our partners are the ones to blame for our unhappiness.

First of all, stop that. Don't give anyone else power over your life and your happiness.

Your partner can't make your happy; the very best they can do is to enhance your happiness. And if there's no happiness within yourself in the first place, there's nothing to enhance (see Chapter 2). You need to take responsibility for any dearth of happiness. The moment you hand over that power to anyone else is the moment that you cease having any control over your life.

You may feel that all the problems and issues you currently are experiencing would dissipate if you were with someone else – and it's true that those particular problems may likely dissipate. They would, however, be replaced by a different set of problems and issues, ones that you would never have considered. Possibly problems and issues that would send you running back to your current partner proclaiming, 'Come back, all is forgiven!'

The point here is not to dwell on it. You could use up a considerable amount of valuable energy and time on this, which could be more productively used elsewhere. The concept of the law of attraction is really pertinent here. In a nutshell (which is what this book is all about), it tells you that, 'Whatever you think about is what you will attract into your life.' Naturally then, if you spend your time thinking about problems, then your life will be full of problems. Everywhere you look you'll see only difficult issues to be resolved.

Why? Because that's where your focus is.

If all you've ever looked for are these problems and issues, then don't be surprised if that's all you find – you'll get what you focus on.

But there are more things for you to take from life, many wonderful opportunities and great experiences just waiting for you. All this is already right here in front of you, but if you're only looking at the negative things in life then you're not going to see (and take) all the wonderful things that you actually want. Do you really want to miss all that life can offer?

Life isn't perfect, there are always going to be some negative things, but you have the power to choose what you absorb. Are you going to constantly lament over all the negative things? Or are you going to push ahead and claim all those things (which are freely available to you right now) that will make your life flourish and bring you the happiness that you crave?

Oh, and incidentally when you choose to take the positive path and fill your life with happiness, suddenly your partner won't seem so bad anymore. In fact, he or she may even start to enhance your happiness. That's all they can do, is to 'enhance'; don't expect anything more than that. They don't have the power to make you happy, in the same way as you don't have the power to make them happy. Your roles are reciprocal, to support, listen to, love and care for one another.

> Remember, you can't help anyone until you are happy within yourself.

Farhan Qureshi

Chapter 7: Be what you want to be; don't wait for permission

There is something that you want to be, but you're currently not. Somewhere inside of you is your real voice, the voice that isn't constrained by the economy, by your need to earn money, by the expectations placed on it by society, by your partner or your boss. But for most of us, that voice stays inside of us and never comes out. We go about our lives thinking, 'If only I could...' Yet we don't do it.

Why is this?

The reasons are vast and complex. It may be that from a young age we were told by a plethora of people not to have such fanciful ideas or that it's silly and that we ought to grow up. What most people do is to go along with it and live their lives according to what others want them to do and to be. They end up one day looking in the mirror, asking themselves, 'What have I done with my life, and why did I spend my life doing what others told me to do ahead of what I really wanted to do?'

There could be other excuses too. Perhaps you felt unsupported by those around you or an event happened that you think prevented you from accomplishing your goals. So many of us, willingly and far too easily, give away power over our lives to someone or something else. But this is the key to changing your mindset. You don't need anyone else's permission to be what you want to be. Stop waiting for someone else's permission – it won't come.

Once you understand that you are in control of your own life, a great obstacle is removed from your path and you can now get on with what you want to spend your life doing.

It's easier to ask for forgiveness than to ask for permission

Related to this is the concept that it's easier to ask for forgiveness than ask for permission.

What does this mean? Simply that if you have an idea for an initiative, just go ahead. If it doesn't work out then just apologise to those people who would otherwise had objected to it (i.e. those who you were looking for permission from). At least you will have tried to accomplish something worthwhile. And of course, when your initiative does succeed then you'll be hailed as a genius from those very same people who'd have blocked your initiative in the first place!

> The only person who you need permission from is yourself.

Chapter 8: The power of saying sorry

In Western culture, being right is seen as a strength, and conversely, being wrong or making mistakes as a sign of weakness. You can see examples of this all around, whether in business, in sport or especially in politics, where politicians very rarely admit to making a mistake, preferring to entrench their positions further, not only insisting that they were right, but that it was everyone else who was wrong.

But since when was being wrong or making a mistake been such a bad thing?

Nobody is perfect; everyone makes mistakes. In fact, one of the differences between average people and great people is that great people will readily admit to making mistakes and not be afraid to say sorry. Great people learn from their mistakes. They change, improve and ultimately move ahead.

Genuinely being sorry has a powerful effect – it's a release mechanism and can free you emotionally from the mistakes of the past and move forwards into the future.

Forgiving others is just as powerful

Next to saying sorry, being able to forgive others (for whatever misdemeanour you perceive them as having done) is the most powerful method of breaking the shackles of the past.

Many of us hold onto events or things (whether intentional or unintentional) that people may have done to us in the past – these are called 'grudges'. But not only does holding a grudge serve no purpose; it actually has a negative effect on your life. Hating other people for what they have done to you (or what you perceive that they have done) is a huge, negative energy source to carry around. Shouldering such a burden limits your potential growth and can serve to push you backwards in life.

In addition, not only will the person against whom you hold a grudge not apologise to you, but oftentimes they're not even aware that they did anything to hurt you in the first place.

So what do you do?

You can wait and wait, but there will be no apology forthcoming. So why not try forgiveness? Make the decision to forgive in your heart (see it as a gift that has contributed to your growth) and move on. Once you have allowed yourself to forgive, you are essentially releasing a shackle that has kept you unnecessarily pinned down.

Always remember that how others live is their issue, not yours.

Let go of the past. You are the only person who has control over the way in which you live your life.

Farhan Qureshi

Chapter 9: We all make mistakes in life, so cut yourself some slack

Following on from the previous chapter about the power of saying sorry and forgiving others, in this chapter we're going to explore forgiveness and making amends.

Whether you should try to make amends for previous mistakes might depend upon the degree of the mistake itself. If it's something irreconcilable, then you may expend more time and energy trying to fix it and ultimately still be unsuccessful. You'll need to use some careful judgement here.

Ultimately, whether you decide to try and mend the issue depends on the importance of the relationship that was damaged. It's unlikely that you can fix a mistake once it's there, and you certainly can't magic it away, but you can work on restoring the damaged relationship. You may need to accept that the relationship will never be completely healed, but you can show the other person/people that you admit your error and are sorry. At the end of the day, you can't force others to forgive you, but you can at least apologise.

One area to consider is whether the mistake was deliberate or not. We all do things which we know are wrong, yet we continue to make mistakes. As you mature, the instances of these errors of judgement will lessen, but they will still occur. The challenge that we all face is whether we are able to control our impulses to do things that we know are wrong. Accept that you're going to fail from time to time and be ready to face up to the consequence of your actions.

Forgive yourself too

Of course, the most important person you can forgive is yourself.

You've made mistakes in the past, some colossal and some minor. Some of those were unintentional errors, and for others you knew perfectly well what you were doing. Rest assured that you're not the only one who's made mistakes. You haven't cornered the market in wrongdoing; everyone does it, everyone falls, everyone fails and everyone gives up.

So cut yourself some slack. You're human and you're meant to make mistakes.

Dealing specifically with the colossal mistakes in your life, it's useful to stop and understand that whatever they were, whoever you hurt and whatever went wrong, they're now in the past and there's nothing you can do about them. There's no time machine to enable you to go back in and alter events. There's no CTRL + Z button.

Remember that you still have the rest of your life to look forwards to. Although you can't change the past, you can certainly decide what you want for your future. Holding onto and reflecting on all the regrets and guilt of the past will keep you there. It will prevent you from moving forwards.

Focus on the future you want, not the past that you can't change.

It's up to you to decide which principles you value most highly; these will be in line with the vision that you have for yourself. The more in tune you are with these valued principles, the more power you'll gain over the impulses to stray from your vision. It's part of growing, but it takes time, so don't expect to be able to just switch it on.

You will continue to make mistakes in the future.

'The only person who doesn't make a mistake is the person who does nothing.'

– Theodore Roosevelt

Farhan Qureshi

PART TWO: YOUR ACTIVITIES

In the previous section, we spoke about the fundamentals of getting your mindset right. In this part of the book, we will move onto more practical advice that you can apply in your day-to-day life.

Chapter 10: Reclaim your life, your 'To Be' list

Whatever it is that is not the way you want it to be, whatever you haven't accomplished yet, anything that is negative in your life is a result of your past best thinking. In the first part of this book we learnt how to change that style of thinking, and now the results you are going to get will be a direct result of your new best thinking.

The first thing to do to reclaim your life is to say, 'Enough is enough. This is not how I want to live my life, and not a second longer am I living like this. I want to change my life and I'm starting now.'

Start living properly. Getting your life in order starts with tidying up yourself, tidying up the home in which you live, getting rid of clutter and things you don't actually need. Now's the time to tidy that sock drawer!

Tidy up your sock drawer? Is this guy serious, I want to change the world here and he's telling me to tidy up my sock drawer?!

Yes, that's what I said. The idea here is to start small. After all, how you going to take on the big things if you can't even get on top of the small ones? These activities should each take under half an hour to do, but their value is that they enable you to change your lifestyle immediately, allowing you to interrupt and break negative patterns that have held you back and move onto more positive patterns that will move you forwards.

You need to live to your ideals, so instead of thinking about how your life 'should be', starting living it that way. Within an hour, your home is already in better order. It's not perfect (it's never going to be, you know), but you have very quickly and easily raised your standards. Your home needs to be a refuge, a place of tranquility for you to attain your higher self – keeping it clean and tidy helps you to find ease and peace. Start with your bedroom and work your way outwards.

When you start to move towards your goal, your goal will start to move towards you. Think of it in steps. Every step you take towards it, it takes a step towards you. Before you know it, your goal will be so close that you'll be within touching distance.

Now that you've got yourself and your home in better order, take the next hour to figure out what you need to do in order to accomplish your goal. Writing it down is always a good idea to make it real. Put your goal header at the top and then start listing out the items you need to do in order to achieve it.

Okay look at your list. Is it that daunting? Is it nearly as lengthy and intimidating as you imagined it to be? Probably not.

Now take a look at the first item on your list and go for it. Keep going for it, again and again, doing whatever you have to do and making whatever sacrifices you have to make to get it done. Don't get distracted (that's why we cleaned up beforehand), and absolutely don't give up until your first task is accomplished.

This may take a while, of course. It could take days or weeks. The idea here isn't to do it in a single sitting. Instead, these individual tasks should be what primarily occupies your time and energy for the next few weeks.

Chunk your time up into months and look through your 'To Be' list (a 'To Be' list is different from a 'To Do' list), and then make a judgement on what is feasible within each month. Plot out the tasks (which become your 'To Do' list) to work on.

As well as your feasible list, set yourself a 'stretch target'. This is what you could do if you stretched even further. Remember that this is all bonus stuff – your feasible list will be the one that determines your success. Going initially for the stretch target will put you off before you begin, so instead focus on the feasible. You'll actually get this done pretty quickly and then you'll have time, energy and motivation to go for the stretch goal too.

You decide what to do here. If you have someone who can hold you accountable, so much so the better.

Chapter 11: What are you waiting for? Do it now!

You'd think that taking action straight away is self-evident, but you'd be surprised at how many people don't understand fundamentally why this is important and what it brings to you in a practical sense.

So let's revisit your 'To Be' list; you should still have it in front of you. We'll now focus on the tasks further down the list. Oftentimes, these are the ones that will require more of your energy, focus and time.

Working hard now, at the beginning of your journey, will buy you more time and declutter your life further down the line so that by that point you will actually have fewer things to do. In this way, you will be more focused and have plenty of energy for the important tasks.

Don't make the mistake of thinking you can go from zero to top speed in a single go. You may be able to massively ramp up on a few occasions, but trying to continuously take massive action will ultimately exhaust and demotivate you. Small steps done more consistently is better than a one-of huge action – the key here is building up that consistency that will ultimately build a wave of momentum, which you then ride towards your goal.

Start setting up those habits, work ethics and muscle memory now. Figure out what it is that you need to do now, step by step. How, in a practical sense, will you complete the task at hand, when will you do it and how often? Building a routine is a good idea. Consider setting up a 21-, 30- or 40-day plan to include your new habit as a regular activity.

> The advantage of setting up a regular system is that not only will your skills be perfectly honed further down the line, but you will also have got most of the 'work' done and out of the way early in the process, leaving you to focus on and enjoy the latter parts of the journey, the point at which it all comes to fruition.

Chapter 12: Urgent versus important activities – how to manage your day

You're very busy and always have loads to do. Life can become overwhelming and although you are constantly running at a hundred percent, at the end of the day you feel as though you haven't moved forwards at all. Why is this? You've worked long and hard all day without a break and yet still there's no progress to show for it.

The answer isn't that you're doing too much; it's because you're doing the wrong things.

There are a whole host of activities in your day that can be usefully split according to two measures:

- Urgency
- Importance

But how can we gauge whether something is 'important' versus 'urgent'? Luckily, there's a simple definition.

'Important' items are those that will have a profound effect on your life. Completing these items are what will give your life the meaning and fulfilment that you're searching for.

'Urgent' items, on the other hand, are those that you think need to be done right now. These don't contribute to your overall vision of yourself at all, like that text message that you feel obliged to instantly check and react to, or being the first to comment on someone's Facebook update.

I'm sure you don't start your day thinking, 'Hey, I really hope I get a non-important interruption from Bob so that I can drop everything to attend to.' Of course not! Yet we let these trivial, 'urgent' interruptions take our time, concentration and energy away from the truly important items in our lives.

In much literature that I've read and many courses that I've attended, the advice is to politely say 'no' to any requests that aren't in your own interests. Personally, I think that's going a bit too far.

I think it's important to help others if there's a genuine request for help. Not only is it the right thing to do ethically, but it will bring you good karma. 'Oh my gosh, he's talking about karma,' I hear you saying. Okay. Hear me out. If you help someone when they need it, then someone will help you out when you need it. It won't necessarily be that same person – don't look for anyone specific to return a favour – but instead it will more likely be a new person who has been drawn to you because of your good nature.

In addition to the 'important' and 'urgent' tasks, there are the self-inflicted time-wasters, things like checking everyone's social media status updates. Did you really need to know what Bob ate for lunch? Unlikely. You certainly didn't need to 'like' or 'comment' on it and then read everyone else's response to your comment! A simple solution is to turn off notifications from social media. In fact, you could even go as far as to not have the app at all, although that will be too extreme for some. But simply turning off the notifications will eliminate a real drain on your valuable time, focus and energy.

The famous Eisenhower Decision Matrix made popular by Stephen Covey in his book The 7 Habits of Highly Effective People is essentially a way to divide your tasks according to their importance. Let's take a look at it in more detail.

	URGENT	NOT URGENT
IMPORTANT	**Quadrant 1** Important and urgent Crises Deadlines Problems	**Quadrant 2** Important but not urgent Relationships Planning Recreation
NOT IMPORTANT	**Quadrant 3** Not important but urgent Interruptions Meetings Activities	**Quadrant 4** Not important and not urgent Time-wasters Pleasant activities Trivia

Here, we can split our tasks out along two axes. Take a moment to think about how your day goes. Are you doing purely 'important' (i.e. Quadrant 2) work or are you caught somewhere between Quadrants 1 and 3 dealing with the crises, interruptions and other people's problems all day long?

If the latter is the case, your day is sure to catch up with you sooner than later, and all the best intentions in the world to stay focused only on important non-urgent items (Quadrant 2) will be very challenging, so accept that you're going to fall short and schedule your time so that the first thing you do is the important stuff.

I now get up early before anyone else can monopolise my time. I use this time to work on stuff that I find really important. Previously, I used to do these tasks last thing at night when all my other activities were done, but I was always too tired, drained and stressed out by the day to really give my important tasks the time, attention and energy they deserved. Now I've switched things around and make my priorities the first things I do.

Try getting up early and do your important tasks straight away. You'll have more energy and no distractions in the morning. See what a difference to your day it makes to know that you have done all your important items before most people have even got out of bed. Not only will it make you feel better and more productive, but you will move quickly towards your goal and ambitions, which will bring true happiness and fulfilment to your life in a way that checking social media updates never will.

Farhan Qureshi

Chapter 13: Drink more water, get more sleep

I can pretty much guarantee you that no matter how much water you are drinking or how much sleep you are getting, you are not getting enough of either right now. Water and sleep are the magic ingredients to give you optimum energy. Far better than any caffeine or sugar fix, much better than any sports drink or energy bar, regular water and adequate sleep will supercharge your day like nothing else, giving you all the positives without any of the side effects.

Let's spend a few seconds looking at the science behind this. Firstly, water.

Water

Two thirds of your body is water, so being properly hydrated not only keeps your blood and circulation clean, it also has incredible benefits for your energy levels and your brain function, both of which need to be at optimum levels to deliver the performance you need to reach your goals.

The long-term benefits of keeping hydrated will keep your organs functioning correctly so that you won't need to spend extra time visiting doctors or hospitals. In fact, generally the more natural food and drink you can have the better.

So how much water should you drink each day?

The quantity of water is dependent upon many factors, including your size, weight, activity levels and even the climate in which you live. Some doctors recommend drinking daily between half an ounce to an ounce (14 to 28 grams) of water for each pound you weigh. So if you weigh 150 pounds, for example, that would be between 75 to 150 ounces of water a day. Obviously if you're in a hotter climate or doing more exercise, then you'd need to be drinking more than that.

Can you drink too much water?

You don't need to go nuts with this. You will know when you are properly hydrated because you will start feeling great and any sugar or caffeine cravings will subside. Another way to tell is that when you go to the toilet, if your urine is clear or very light yellow and has little odour then you're well hydrated.

A few quick changes you can make right now to make sure you get enough water:

- Always carry a bottle of water with you – make sure it's fresh and clean every day.

- Drink a whole glass of water when you wake up – you will be dehydrated after a night's sleep, so instead of rushing for coffee, drink water.

- If you fancy a coffee or soda, first have a bottle or glass of water. After about five minutes, see whether you still want the caffeinated drink. Chances are you won't be so thirsty anymore.

- Keep sipping throughout the day – it's better to drink water slowly and consistently rather than in one go.

Sleep

The other essential element in supercharging your day is sleep. Because we have so many demands on us, this can be tougher to crack, but treat getting adequate sleep as a priority. If you can't get enough sleep every night, schedule some nights when you will go to bed early – I'd recommend at least twice a week, perhaps Sunday (to set you up for the work/school week) and Thursday (to set you up for the weekend), but do whatever works for you.

If you combine getting enough sleep with putting your most important items at the start of the next day, you will really boost your productivity and energy levels. Sleep can often be overlooked, but nobody should feel that they are too busy to get enough sleep. Really, what could be more important than your health?

Yet oddly, it's often the unimportant time-wasting activities (those that have no health benefits) that contribute to our lack of sleep. Compare how many times you've delayed going to bed because you were doing something genuinely important versus the times that social media and other mobile/online/television activity kept you from getting to bed on time.

I'm not saying never to indulge in this, but just give yourself a break from it from time to time. Not only will you be able to use your energy to get your important items done, but when you've accomplished much of your 'To Be' list, you can balance out your time on these other activities – after all, we all need some faffing-around time. Just don't let it dominate your life.

> Your task? Drink plenty of water and get adequate sleep for the remainder of this week. See how much better you feel and how much more you accomplish.

Chapter 14: Would you rather have pain or regret?

The choice of being successful or not boils down to whether you go for your dream or let it drift away. The first option may involve what you perceive to be a lot of pain and discomfort (we'll debunk that in a couple of paragraphs) but the second option of letting your dream go will involve regret.

Essentially your choice is between:

- perceived pain and discomfort, which is temporary, or
- regret which will last forever

Make no mistake about it, you are choosing one or the other right now. If you think you aren't or you think that you haven't made a choice, then in reality you have already chosen 'regret'.

People often ask me how do I do all the things that I manage to do, yet the truth is that I'm no better than anyone else. I'm not better disciplined or more organised, but I really hate regret. I can't live with knowing that I didn't do something I could have done.

That sort of regret tends to eat away at me. I imagine it does with a lot of people.

If you're already in pain, why not push yourself and work hard to get out of it? Why not get something from it rather than constantly living with it? We spoke in Chapter 4 about societal expectations holding us back and in Chapter 7 about not needing permission from those around us. Those factors numb our pain and keep us where we are, but ultimately, when we look back on our lives, we won't be able to go back and change anything. Today, on the other hand, we can.

You can change your life now. You can choose not to have any more regrets.

On the topic of pain, there are three things to remember. Firstly pain is simply a case of perception, and is only really the discomfort that you feel about change. It may be that you need to change something about yourself, about your routines, about the people you are spending most of your time with – whatever the change is, it's this that causes us discomfort, rather than the actual activity in hand. Once you make positive change, then your new elevated situation becomes the norm and you forget about any of the old comfort that you used to draw upon. In fact, you may start to wonder how you even lived like that in the first place.

Secondly, pain is temporary. Success, on the other hand, is permanent. Once you achieve whatever it is that you're dreaming about, it's there, it's manifested, no one can take that achievement away from you and the pain is long forgotten.

And finally, you only feel pain when you think about doing your task. Once you get into the action itself, you start getting fulfilment and actually find enjoyment and fun in the process.

So get up and get over the initial discomfort. The treasure you seek is in the cave that you fear to enter.

Farhan Qureshi

Chapter 15: Choose how you spend your 'own' time

An interesting theory about work is that after the financial compensation, people's main reason for going to work is to gain satisfaction and to fulfil their potential. But how many people actually do jobs that they are interested in, jobs that they want to do? Do you? Do you find your work interesting and fulfilling, or are you doing it merely to earn money?

The sad truth is that most people are currently employed in jobs that they are not totally satisfied doing. There are varied reasons for this, and some are perfectly genuine and noble, for example a parent who does a job because it pays the bills and keeps a roof over their family's head. There are other people who may even have had to sacrifice doing their dream job to pursue a different line of work, a line of work that pays more or one that has better job security.

But there are also less valid reasons, like being scared, not being brave enough to go for what you want. These reasons are common and understandable.

Whatever situation you find yourself in, any given job is going to demand more of your time than the contracted hours state. The question is whether doing those extra hours and going that extra mile is a worthwhile investment of your time.

If you are already in your dream job, then definitely going that extra mile will be worthwhile, not only because of the possibility of being rewarded/recognised but because it gives you intense satisfaction. But if on the other hand you're not doing something you care deeply about, then ask yourself whether that extra time could be better invested elsewhere.

When you have met all your obligations, be discerning about which extra activities you choose to commit to. Don't feel pressured into giving up your own time to do something that you don't want to do. Fine at work, work rules apply, but in your own time, your own rules apply.

Identify any skills gaps that exist between your current job and your ideal job. Use your spare time to plug those gaps and move yourself to the position you want to be in.

If you've got children, I would recommend spending your non-work time with them, especially when they are young. Clichéd though it might seem, this time period will pass all too quickly, and being able to reflect back on all the great times you had when they were children will be far more satisfying than remembering that great spreadsheet you sacrificed a summer's evening for.

On the subject of working hours, there's a real old-school macho attitude of 'look-how-many-hours-I-do-a-week' that is quite pervasive in our society. People will happily boast about the number of extra hours that they work. It's worth remembering that whatever you do at work is what you'll become known for. Would you like to be known as the person who's first in and last out, the type of person who works all hours? Or would you prefer to be recognised as the expert, the go-to person who knows the answers and can also maintain a healthy and successful work-life balance?

Who do you think works more hours and who do you think has more credibility – the person who works for longer and gets less done or the person who works sensible hours and gets more done? I know which one I'd choose.

> Define how you want to be known, and then stick to it. There may be some initial resistance if you don't fit an expected mould, but in the long-term, people will respect you more and value the contribution you bring to a team.

Farhan Qureshi

Chapter 16: Control – where are you placing your focus?

Control is one of the great signifiers of success in our modern age. To have control over events, over people, over companies, over societies and over outcomes is considered the highest form of achievement. If you have it, society deems you a success; without it, you are viewed as an abject failure.

But control is really an illusion.

The truth is that we don't have any real control over what goes on in our lives. We can't control the economy, our jobs, the weather or how well our favourite sports teams fare. Most, if not everything, is out of our control. But there is something that we do have control over. And it's the most important thing of all. Most significantly we do have control over ourselves. We are able to control how we think, how we behave, what our actions and responses are in any given circumstance, and we have that control all of the time.

However, some of us give away that control all too readily, perhaps blaming those around us for our situation. Some give away that control to the circumstances we find ourselves in, blaming the government, the economy or the fact that we're tired and hungry.

You probably know a lot of people who do this. And you're probably guilty of it yourself from time to time. But you don't have to be that person. Instead, you can take control over the most important asset you have.

Your ability to control what you think is fundamental to your behaviour. What you think directly impacts what you do, and the choices that you make are more powerful than any economic factors, more powerful than any force of nature, more powerful than any company rejecting your CV or laying you off. Your ability to control yourself is what will drive you to success ahead of any extrinsic factor.

Your inner reality creates your outer reality

Imagine a company goes bankrupt and all the employees lose their jobs. Some people will lament their losses, whilst others will spend their energy blaming the management who led them to this situation. These groups of people will not get anywhere. It's the third group of people who will move forward, those who accept that they had no control over what others did. This group of people are smart enough to know not to expend any energy on the failings of others or to dwell on the past. They know that their energy is better spent in finding a new job. In the case of a whole industry failing, this group of empowered people realise quickly that they need to re-invent themselves and learn new skills and strategies. All the time they are focused on what they can do to make their situation better, controlling their emotions and performance – they don't give their power away to anyone else.

If you are facing hardship, the first step you can take to get out of it is to take back control over yourself and never, ever give it away.

There will, of course, be tough times; it's part of the game. The question is, are you going to give control away to someone else or will you hold onto one of your most powerful assets?

Farhan Qureshi

PART THREE: HARNESSING THE WORLD AROUND YOU

You may think that you are on your way to easy success now that you know about your mindset and have learnt how to plan and execute your day. Well you're almost there. But family members, work colleagues, friends and the world in general is going to continue to seemingly conspire against you – it's par for the course. This section is going to prepare you to meet those challenges.

Farhan Qureshi

Chapter 17: The secret of win-win: seek first to understand

The number one take-away advice I have drawn from many years of studying and practising in the field of self-help, is that to improve your relationships and accomplish more in the world you need to 'seek first to understand before being understood' (from Stephen Covey's exceptional tome The 7 Habits of Highly Effective People; in fact it is habit number 5).

Put simply, you will achieve what you want and be better able to influence the outcomes you want when working with others. Working collaboratively brings about a synergy which allows you to reach further than you ever could on your own.

Working together means trying to empathise with other people, trying to genuinely appreciate and understand their perspectives, concerns, issues and reservations. When you understand this and put yourself in their shoes, you are able to shape a proposal or plan that works for both of you.

When you can do this effectively, you will meet with less resistance and foster increased co-operation within your relationships, with other people helping you to achieve a better result.

So how do you actually do this?

Although the premise sounds fairly straightforward, many of us run into trouble in building and maintaining successful relationships.

Think about when you're meeting a new person, be it at a cocktail party, a networking event or a chance meeting. How often do you forget that person's name mere seconds after they told you? Most of us don't even hear the name in the first place, since we are too busy focusing on our own objectives – what we are going to say, how we are going to introduce ourselves and what we want out of the encounter. That is how we fail at the first hurdle.

Building on that thought, when you want to pitch an idea or proposal to others, first listen to what they want out of it. Think, 'What's in it for them? What's in it for me?' It has to come from a win-win viewpoint, which can only happen if you first understand, 'What's in it for them?'

There's an old story of two sisters fighting over an orange. Both sisters want the fruit and scream and fight over it until they are blue in the face. Finally, their mother has enough of the incessant fighting. She takes the orange, peels it, throws the peel away, and gives half to each sister. But still the crying continues. The mother can't understand. After all, they each have half and the problem has been solved fairly. Only when she asks her daughters why they are still upset does she discover that one sister wanted the orange rind for her cake and the other wanted to squeeze the juice.

> Don't presuppose that you know the answer; first listen to the question.

Farhan Qureshi

Chapter 18: Why you shouldn't compare yourself to others and how to stop doing it

Whether consciously or sub-consciously, you probably have been measuring yourself against others, judging your success versus how well others are doing or have done in the past. This isn't necessarily your fault, but is something that you've been experiencing since childhood. Maybe you were compared to a sibling or other children at school – even today, school reports, staff appraisals and team selections still operate from these modi operandi.

But you can make a choice and stop any unnecessary comparison. In the words of Homer (Simpson), 'It doesn't matter how good you are at something – there's always a million people better than you at it.'

You are tested according to your strengths – because you're strong (you wouldn't be reading this otherwise) you then have more responsibility to achieve. Your life isn't for frittering away; you have a greater purpose.

So here are some truths that you might like to consider when you compare yourself to anyone else:

- Everyone had a different starting position. You don't know how much of a head start someone else has had over you.

- Others may get more help than you. Although it may appear superficially that someone else has accomplished much on their own, you don't know how much help they have been given behind the scenes.

- Everyone is at a different stage in their life.

- You don't really know what goes on in other people's lives. Publicly all may seem well, but what's happening behind closed doors may not be as brilliant as it seems.

- You don't know what's next for that person (or for yourself).

Don't get bitter when you see others who have more than you. When you see someone else get a nice new house or posting photos at an exclusive holiday resort, don't waste your time and energy wondering how they have achieved this so easily. Instead, wish them the best and be happy for them. After you've done your well-wishing, then focus on yourself. Focus exclusively on what you can do.

Interestingly enough, there's a lot of research that points to the fact that those who are constantly posting on social media about just how great their lives are, are those people who are less intrinsically happy. So don't spend your precious time and energy focusing on others. Simply wish them well and carry on.

Finally, do yourself a favour avoid posting about your life on social media. Instead, go out and live your life! Accomplish the things you want to do and become that person that others will post about.

Farhan Qureshi

Chapter 19: Choose your friends carefully

The famous motivational speaker Jim Rohn coined the great phrase, 'You are the average of the five people you spend the most time with.'

Mathematically it may not be entirely provable, but the concept here is that the people with whom you chose to spend most of your time will be those whose influence rubs off on you the most.

The company you choose goes beyond just physical habit-forming. It fundamentally affects the way in which you see the world and the decisions you subsequently make.

If you spend all your time with negative people who always see the worst in everything and constantly let their cynicism prevent them from taking any opportunities, then you too will have a negative outlook on life. This is partly due to our need to be socially accepted, as we look for validation from our peers.

I'm not advocating that you cut yourself off entirely from anyone who isn't your perfect choice of companion. After all, we may have family members or old friends who have been very loyal and who possess these traits. But by limiting your time with negative people and instead going out and finding groups of people to whom you aspire, you will build a network of friends who are inspirational and motivating.

Ask yourself what kind of person you want to be. Are the five people you spend the most time with currently contributing to that ideal? If not, just reduce the time you spend with them.

For me, I experienced this first when I enrolled in a creative writing class. I was surrounded by other writers who would write the most amazing stories I had ever heard. I was so energised from being around them. I then went on to join various filmmaking clubs and surrounded myself with filmmakers. I immersed and surrounded myself with so many creative people that it's hardly surprising that that was the most creative and productive time of my life.

I would encourage you to go and seek out groups of people who you aspire to become; they're easier to find than you might think. And if you can't find them or make contact with them, you can still spend time in their realm by reading books, finding podcasts and joining online forums in those areas – these are valid ways to spend time with those groups, absorb their ideas and tune into the same wavelength that they operate from.

Chapter 20: What if you don't have anyone to support you?

This is slightly different to the concept of choosing your friends carefully, which we covered in the previous chapter. Although you can have an empathetic circle of friends who inspire you to reach your goals, this chapter is more about having an actual support network in place, a network that can help you achieve those goals.

Let's face it, our individual goals are unique and in many cases contain nuances that those around us won't generally understand. Our immediate circles may wonder why we continuously pound into dead ends when there are easier and more conventional ways to make money.

So you need to really find a network of collaborators who can help you, who can provide you with resources, interaction and hold you accountable to do what it is that you say you will do. These groups are relatively easy to find using online resources such as social media groups. In fact, one of the best things about social media is the communities centred around certain interests. You should use these online resources and communities as much as you can. Don't forget too, though, that they are not a replacement for real social contact, so do actually try meeting people face-to-face. The meetup website http://www.meetup.com/ is an excellent resource to find people in the same location as yourself.

Typically, in these groups you will find three types of people:

1. people who are at a more advanced level than you
2. people who are at the same level as you
3. people who are at a less advanced level than you

You'll need to work with these three groups and form networks with them in different ways.

Naturally you will feel that you can gain most from the first group (i.e. people who are at a more advanced level than you) but what is it that they have to gain from networking with you? If someone is at the top of their game, they may well have hundreds of people making demands on their time. Do they really need another person? By all means aim to make connections with this group as they can really help you, but in reality expect a small proportion of these people to assist you with practical help.

The second group (people at the same level as you) is where the bulk of your network will be formed. This is where you can all help each other, and these people will be expecting you to help them as much as they help you. Think of this as this is your year group at school; you will all be learning and moving upwards together. Really try to get involved as much as you can with this group. Arrange to meet outside of the group and set targets to which you will hold each other accountable. Make sure that you can find a small group that will commit to meeting regularly and reviewing each other's work.

The third group (people who are at an earlier level than you) you may initially think can't offer you much. But remember how the first group shunned you because you couldn't offer them much? Was there someone from that group who did give you time and attention? Now it's your turn to pay that forwards to the third group. It's in this third group where you will find those who will work hardest and put in the longest hours; they are the hungriest and most eager. Invest some time in this group, coach and mentor them as best as you can. It's unlikely that they'll receive much attention from the first group and if they are genuinely committed to the skill at hand, it won't be long until they are the same level as you.

Farhan Qureshi

Chapter 21: Stop trying to be right all the time

On the theme of wasting time and energy, trying to be right all the time is one of the biggest wasters there is.

What do you actually even win if you convince others that you are right? Are you going to change their behaviour? It's highly unlikely. Even if you could convince someone else that you are right, what do you gain out of it? Is the effort to change someone else's viewpoint worth the time and energy you expend? Could you have used your time and energy better, perhaps on yourself?

The whole world is a rich tapestry of different thoughts and opinions. But despite this wonderful diversity, you will see many people trying to unify thought and opinion, typically to their own. When they do this, they lose all sense of breadth and variety in thought and the resulting outcome becomes mediocre. Much better to go the other way and celebrate such richness in thought. Diversity amongst us brings greater outcomes for both individuals and groups.

In fact, you can feed off this plurality of thought to enhance your ability to generate ideas and solutions. The more ideas there are in the melting pot, the wider the set of solutions there are to choose from. Why would anyone want to narrow the range of ideas and solutions available to them?

When someone else is trying to convince you that they are right

So what about the flip side, when someone is trying to convince you that you are wrong and that you need to move over to their way of thinking?

Should you resist and put your case forward or should you just smile, nod and move away?

The answer depends on the situation in hand. If you're speaking to some random stranger whom you're unlikely to see again and who has no bearing on the results that you can achieve, don't waste your energy and time fighting them. Just smile politely and don't give it another thought. It means nothing to you.

But what if it's someone on whose relationship you count upon? Perhaps it's a partner or boss, where you have a stake in the outcome.

In these situations, then you need to adopt a solution-oriented mindset. Start by listening to their concerns and trying to understand. Once you truly comprehend and can demonstrate that you understand, will you be able to come up with answers that meet both your criteria. A joint solution that benefits both parties will be met with less resistance and it will help build a stronger relationship.

It's this relationship-building that is really important. You and your partner/boss could both be right about a particular issue but by working together, you can create a synergy from your solution and theirs. The 'win' here isn't just limited to the particular case in question. What you're actually doing is building trust and the ability to create a series of better 'win-win' solutions (see Chapter 17) further down the line.
This is so much more beneficial to both parties than spending all your valuable time and energy on simply proving your point.

Farhan Qureshi

Chapter 22: Everything happens for a reason

There are lessons that life serves us, and when we are wise enough to recognise that what we perceive as negative situations can actually be opportunities in disguise, we can start to claim back the power for our success and not give it away cheaply. These situations serve to make us greater people. There's a very famous Urdu poem that roughly translates to:

> 'Dear Eagle don't be afraid of the strong winds, they only serve to make you soar higher.'
> – Sayyed Sadiq Hussain Shah

You are that eagle.

In fact, one of the most important ideas that will help you deal with the world around you is to understand that everything happens for a reason, whether you like it or not. Coming to terms with this fact will help you to free yourself from the counterfactual thinking that holds so many of us back in life.

So what is counterfactual thinking?

Counterfactual thinking is when we think that our current situation would have been different if only we had made a different decision earlier. You could have missed a flight and then spent your time wondering what would have happened if you'd left 30 mins earlier, taken a different route, or finished packing the night before... The list is never-ending. As well as wasting a lot of time and energy, counterfactual thinking doesn't solve your problem and it prevents you from coming up with a solution.

You can't control outcomes but you can control your inputs

Essentially the concept here is that you can't control whatever your desired output is, but you do have full control over what you put into achieving your goals. For example, a few months back I made a Minecraft YouTube video (http://bit.ly/megaminecraft). My aim was to get a million views on YouTube. After all, I've seen others videos do it, so I figured I could do it too.

In reality, I have no control on whether I get a million views or not. There are so many factors involved in getting a million views, some of which are out of my control (YouTube SEO (Search Engine Optimisation) updates, visibility of my video in related videos, whether a user types 'Minecraft' into the search box, the list goes on) and some of which are entirely within my control.

I focused on the things I did have control over, things like:

- making the video
- editing and doing sound design
- designing a great poster
- uploading it to YouTube
- posting on all types of social media and
- telling people about it who may be interested

In any given task, the things that you do control will often precede the things that you don't have control over. In my case, YouTube SEO can't kick in unless I make and upload a video to YouTube in the first place.

> There are a lot of things you can control. The question is. 'Will you still work hard to complete your tasks despite how tough and bleak the situation might seem?' This will show how much you really want it.
>
> Do you really want it or do you kind-of-want-it-so-long-as-it's-not-too-difficult?

Farhan Qureshi

Chapter 23: Talk ideas, not people

It is crazy how much time people put into trying to control others, and the amount of energy they put into criticising and analysing how other people's lives would be better if only they did A, B or C.

Don't be that person. If you are that person, stop it immediately – you are wasting your time and energy.

We are exposed to an inordinate amount of gossiping, with people constantly discussing and criticising those around them. Think for a moment about the people you know who engage in those types of activity.

- Are they the type of people who move ahead?
- Are they the type who have achieved great success in their lives?
- Do you want to be like those people?

What do you gain from discussing other people? Not only do you not gain anything – after all, that other person is unlikely to change and most of the time they're not even present – but fixating on others won't move you any closer to your goals. You have better things to do.

One of the idioms I grew up with was:

> 'Great minds discuss ideas,
> average minds discuss events,
> small minds discuss people.'
>
> – Eleanor Roosevelt

We even had this printed and hung on the wall in our living room. I think the quote is great. The more time you can spend on talking about and actioning 'ideas' (preferably your own), the richer your life becomes.

Everyone is on a journey in life and we are all at a different stage on that journey. This is not necessarily linked to age; there are many other factors involved as we progress. Focus on your journey and if you really want to influence others, do it through leading by example. Inspire others by being the success that you want to be – it sure beats nagging and griping about others. Who wants to hear that?

Make no mistake about it, your outer world is a reflection of what goes on in your mind. Do you want your life to be dominated by the faults and misbehaviour of others or do you want your life to be full of the ideas, visions and dreams you have for yourself?

Think ideas and work with other people on theirs. You can learn a lot from them, how they fill their lives with dreams and plans, and the work patterns and discipline they use to make their ideas come true. Then use those techniques to bring your own ideas to life.

Are you inspired by people badgering you or by people who have achieved the greatness that you desire?

Farhan Qureshi

Chapter 24: You catch more bees with honey than with vinegar

So many people think they can get what they want from others by shouting, screaming and manipulating to get their own way. But be it at work or even at home, the results gained from shouting are limited and flawed. When people do things out of fear of you, they will do the bare minimum to complete the task, and it will be slow, sloppy and incomplete. That's if they finish it at all.

However, being nice to people, taking time to understand them first (see Chapter 23) and not trying to always be right the whole time (see Chapter 21) changes the whole paradigm of 'interdependent' relationships.

The manager who is always harsh gets her team to complete her orders. She may get her deliverable completed, but it won't be particularly high quality, and may well have hidden flaws that will surface later. This is because the team did what she said out of fear. There's no space or willingness in this team to flag potential problems or offer better solutions because they know that the manager will be inflexible and just start screaming.

In contrast, the same team but with a manager who wins her team's trust, who listens to her team, who values her team and her team's happiness, will make the deliverable exceptional. They will never need to be asked to put in extra effort or hours, but will do this willingly. This is the team who will spot potential blockers and take remedial action without needing to be prompted or expecting material reward.

Two identical teams under different leadership styles will perform differently.

The same philosophy holds true in the home. Contrast the harsh parent, who without any imagination shouts at their children to get a household chore done. They think that results can only be achieved by shouting. Okay yes, the children brush their teeth, get ready for school on time etc. But they're only carrying out these tasks because they don't want to be shouted at. They don't understand why it's important to clean their teeth or what the health benefits are and almost certainly when the parent isn't there to shout at them, they won't do it at all.

Whenever you are in a potential confrontational situation, just start with a smile and a soft tone. This is usually enough to totally disarm the other party. Using this technique, I've avoided parking fines, potential road rage from other drivers and made friends with otherwise difficult neighbours and bosses.

Instead of telling people to just do things, explain the 'why' behind your request and ask them for their opinion on the best way to achieve a solution. Now you're putting them in the position of an expert. As they probe into the solution, they'll come to see that they are the person who can solve it best and they will take ownership. Giving people ownership empowers them.

As a boss, leader or parent, empowering others is one of the most important things you can do, allowing teams, organisations and families to be able to look after themselves. Subsequently, they need less of your day-to-day management time and will do a better job when using their own initiative.

Doesn't that sound good, having teams, families and even communities that can look after themselves? Wouldn't you feel freer, and wouldn't you progress further if you could strategise, plan and work towards the goals you have in your life, rather than having to manage the minutiae in other people's lives?

> A little kindness goes a long way.

Farhan Qureshi

Chapter 25: Talk to those who've been there

Getting advice from others is often a great idea. Some advice you will agree with, some of it will make you question. 'Why did that person say that? Are they trying to sabotage my efforts? Maybe they're just jealous.' You may feel that you're in competition with people in your own age range and peer group, and you may be right. But it's important to always be open to listening to new ideas, especially those that don't match your own. This is where you will challenge your own ideas and maybe come up with a better way.

There are a group of people whose advice you may easily dismiss, and that is people of an older generation than yourself, perhaps your parents, grandparents or an older boss. On the surface you may think, 'What do they know? The world has changed so many times since they were my age.'

Undoubtedly the world has changed. Technology has progressed, working patterns have adjusted, gender roles have shifted, property prices to earnings ratios have massively shot up – indeed a lot has changed.

But the world and society in general is still built on the same foundations that were laid many hundreds and thousands of years ago; those things haven't changed. Although we may receive multimedia messages on phones instead of plain text via telegrams, the fundamentals still apply – the top cosmetic layer may be different but the core remains.

While we are currently fixated on that top layer of cool technology and virtualisation, we think that somehow we know it all. But by focusing so much on the foreground, we tend to lose perspective of an all-pervasive background. We can't see the wood for the trees.

Older people have that wider view. We are right in the thick of it whereas they are able to stand back and see the situation play out. It's rather like when a football manager watches the first half from the stand. As a player you're right in the midst of the game, but the manager in the stand can see the whole situation unfolding. From this different perspective (and from having done it before), he can see things that you can't.

On the surface, the problems you face today may seem completely different from the problems older people faced in the past, but below the surface, there are echoes of either the challenges that you face or the opportunities that you are letting pass by. The same fundamental set of universal truths are playing themselves out again.

There is extreme value in older people's advice, value that is all but absent in today's media and advertising. Our older generations are one of our greatest assets. They've gone through challenges and horrors that we will hopefully never have to endure. Take that wisdom and harness it in your life while it is still here, and learn through their experiences – they made it, survived, even thrived through their challenges, and you will make it through yours.

Talk to younger people too. Again, they will have a different perspective on life than you. It may be that they ask you a lot of 'What if?' questions and are more open to exploring ideas. Their view of the world will certainly be different to yours, and it's these different perspectives that will challenge and ultimately improve your own.

> Whatever form wisdom comes in, young or old, grasp it.

Farhan Qureshi

PART FOUR: MAKING IT REAL

In this final part of the book you will take everything you've learnt so far, put it all together and blend it so that you can start living your dream life.

Farhan Qureshi

Chapter 26: Create a vision board

So now comes the time to pull everything together, but what is it that you are actually making real? Do you even know what it is that you want to create? How will you know if you're progressing, if you're getting closer or even if you've arrived at the destination you want?

A vision board is a simple concept and it's actually great fun to make. Essentially, it comprises of a board (could be a book, a piece of paper or a mobile app) where you collect pictures/text of what you want.

Many people get confused and take the attitude that vision boards are a wish list of things they want to own or possess. But it's not about having; it's about being.

Start with yourself. What do you want to be? See yourself in your true light.

What does the real you look like?

How does the real you speak like, dress and live? Yes, you will be putting down pictures of nice houses, nice cars, nice clothes, but all these material items are just a means to an end. Remember that the items are not the goal. Rather it's about you living to the highest standards that you choose to envision.

Be very specific here. The more specific you are, the clearer your goal becomes. When it stops becoming vague, what you are actually doing is tuning into the frequency that will bring your dream lifestyle to you.

One of the basic laws of attraction is to do with vibrational frequency. You operate on a frequency, as does everything else, and when you tune into that frequency, opportunities, events, people and serendipity start appearing (the technical term is 'manifesting') in your life.

This is no accident.

The vision board is a fun way of actually tuning into the right frequency and allowing things to come to you. Notice I didn't say it's your target. The precise goal of the vision board is to become a receiver. Obviously there's a degree of work to be done and nothing just magically turns up without putting some effort in. But going through this process and gaining clarity will open up channels and pathways to you ultimately receiving what you want.

Display your board in a prominent place, somewhere where you can see it regularly. Not only will this help you re-tune on a daily basis, but it will also help you when you need it most, when things feel unbearably tough, when you're exhausted, miserable and about to give up. That's when your vision board will get you back on track. That's when you remember that you (i.e. your true self) created it and that the tiredness, the pain and the heartache you're feeling at any given moment is only transient. Use your vision board to get past these temporary feelings and tune yourself back to the real you.

> See it, plan for it, act towards it. It all starts with your vision for yourself.

Farhan Qureshi

Chapter 27: So what if it's difficult? Do it anyway!

Like the changing seasons of spring, summer and autumn, there will be times of beauty, fun and happiness in your life. But there will also be a winter, a time when life is going to be tough. There will be barren spells, times where nothing works, where everything you do fails and when people turn their backs on you.

So what should you do in times of adversity? Give up and start crying?

The first step to being able to navigate the difficult times is to know that everyone experiences these times, that at some point the waters will become choppy. Although it won't avoid it completely, being prepared will at least soften the shock.

Adversity doesn't last forever and just as spring follows winter, so ease and growth follows hardship. Accepting this will allow you to turn those difficult times around. Instead of merely 'surviving', you will be able to 'thrive' and 'cultivate' during these periods.

This is where the real progress in your life will occur. Anyone can achieve when times are easy, when everything is going your way and when everyone is supporting you. But can you do it when times are hard?

If you can keep going when it's difficult, when it's cold, when you're tired and hungry, you will make the biggest progress in your life and jump up to the next plateau.

The pain that you feel will only be temporary. After you've completed and gone through it, you'll come out the other side a much stronger person. In fact, some of those very tasks and periods of time that you so despised are the ones that form you. Much like a diamond is forged under pressure, so your dreams turn into reality when you power through the difficult periods in your life.

The reason for this is that when things are easy and comfortable, we tend to just talk about our dreams, and there's nothing actually driving us to make them real. One technique to move yourself out of difficult times is to attach so much pain to your predicament that you physically force and drive yourself out of it.

The brain dislikes pain and will do anything it can to get out of a painful situation. By attaching a level of pain to your current situation, you will give yourself no choice other than to take action. It's almost like having to kickstart and get yourself into gear. It's the pain that will get the whole process moving, and then the hunger that keeps you moving.

Your current reality is a result of your current best thinking. Put another way, your best thinking has gotten you to your current position.

If you want to change your life, begin by changing your thinking. Then your next reality becomes a product of that better thinking. Somewhat unfortunately, the shift that you need to make is borne out of the difficulties that you face currently (see Chapter 22 – Everything happens for a reason).

The next step is to continue to drive your life forwards. Don't wait to hit hard times before you take massive action. Continuing to push yourself as you start achieving your dreams requires emotional maturity. The opposite of emotional maturity is to become complacent; complacency will actually send your life backwards.

Having emotional maturity, on the other hand, will enable you to fulfil all your current dreams and continue to make your dreams bigger as you continue to grow.

The wolf climbing the hill is hungrier than the wolf already at the top.

> Once you achieve your current goal, dream another one, dream a bigger one, continue to grow – keep yourself hungry for more.

Farhan Qureshi

Chapter 28: Step outside the complacent zone

Quite likely you've heard of the term 'comfort zone'. It's that lifestyle that keeps you stuck in your current situation. You don't move for fear of upsetting your nice, easy routine. Perhaps you'll watch a motivational video or listen to an inspiring podcast and that gets you all fired up. You decide to do something about it, make some kind of change and then suddenly, you're out of your comfort zone.

Well you are out of your comfort zone now. More than that, you've actually moved into a more dangerous zone, one that fools you into thinking you're making progress – this zone is called the 'complacent zone', and it's actually a more dangerous place to be.

Why is this?

Well firstly we all know when we're in our comfort zone and we all know that we should move out of it. In contrast, we seldom recognise when we're in the complacent zone. In fact, most people don't even know that this zone exists.

The complacent zone is the zone you are in where you think you're making progress, where you're trying really hard, you're pushing yourself and believing that you going to make some progress. It's all effort with no result and ultimately forces you to give up and vow never to try again. That's because in this zone you are just burning out your energy without a clear plan of what you're doing. It's like a football team that thinks if they just keep running they will win the game – they won't. At best they'll get a draw.

The teams and individuals that win are those with a plan. Once they have the plan they then use their effort to execute that plan. The team that knows where and how to attack, when to hold, when to run, when to go short, when to go long is the team that wins.

So do something every day that scares you. Push yourself beyond your limits. But just make sure that you have some kind of objective before you do these things. Set milestones that you want to hit, rather than aimlessly going from one big hairy, scary goal to the next.

Stepping outside of your comfort zone is a cliché that will make you feel better about yourself but won't get you any closer to your goal. Make a plan of how you're going to achieve your goal and then apply your effort in that direction to move you outside your complacent zone.

The treasure you seek is in the cave that you are afraid to venture in. Be smart and step outside your complacent zone. Go after the dream you are harbouring. You may perceive that you've either succeeded or failed, but in reality the latter is true, since you are now outside your complacent zone.

Farhan Qureshi

Chapter 29: You don't need anyone's approval

So you've figured out what it is you want to do, you've put your vision board together, you've psyched yourself up, you've even planned out your schedule, but for some reason you don't move.

What's stopping you from going out and getting results? You're at the start line and the starting pistol's fired, but you're not running.

Don't worry, the same thing happens to all of us. What you're doing is looking around, waiting for someone else's approval, for someone to cheer you on, give you a kiss before you go or tell you how proud they are of you before you embark on your adventure.

Guess what? You'll be waiting a long time for that.

It's not that people are deliberately cruel, or that they don't care enough to wish you 'bon voyage', but just that everyone is lost in their own little world, pre-occupied with their own life. What's important to you may not be important to them. In fact, more likely is that it's not even on their radar – don't take it personally.

The thing we need to get ourselves out of this inertia is to stop waiting for people's approval and permission. Just go ahead and do it.

And by the way, don't expect people to support you on your adventure or even congratulate you when you succeed. Remember that you are not doing this to win anyone else's approval. If you are doing this to impress anyone else, then you are truly setting yourself up for disappointment – stop it right now.

Remember in Chapter 7 when we said that now is the time to do this on your own? Don't expect your friends or family to come along with you for the ride. On this journey you will start to meet new friends. These new friends are there to help you and cheer you on. Why? Because they share the same vision as you. They will help you plough the new ground. It's in these new friendships that you will find new meaning.

Even then, don't expect or wait for your new friends to approve everything you do. Everyone comes into your life for a reason. Some of these people will be there to encourage and inspire you, others will be there for course correction, to challenge you and teach you something that you weren't able to learn on your own. They won't all be around forever, but that's okay.

Embrace this change as you move into the new. It will be scary, you may want to give up and more than likely you will have to do a lot of this on your own. Don't forget that you have everything within you to do this. You wouldn't have this ambition if you weren't able to accomplish it. It's down to you to draw within your own reserves of intelligence, talent and courage.

> It's because you already have all the attributes that you can do this. All you need to do now is give yourself permission. The only approval you need is from yourself.

Farhan Qureshi

Chapter 30: How to use the Pareto 80:20 rule in your favour

The Pareto principle is based on the idea that 80% of effects come from 20% of causes. Management consultant Joseph M. Juran suggested the principle and named it after Italian economist Vilfredo Pareto, who, while at the University of Lausanne in 1896, published his first paper 'Cours d'économie politique'. Essentially, Pareto showed that approximately 80% of the land in Italy was owned by 20% of the population; Pareto developed the principle by observing that 20% of the pea pods in his garden contained 80% of the peas.

This 80:20 rule has been observed in many areas of science, in business (80% of problems can be attributed to 20% of causes or 80% of a company's profits come from 20% of its customers), in software (Microsoft noted that by fixing the top 20% of the most-reported bugs, 80% of the related errors and crashes in a given system would be eliminated), and in many other fields.

The point here is that you can use this to your advantage. Instead of thinking that you have to do everything on your to-do list, just focus and prioritise the most important things. Remember this quadrant diagram from Chapter 12?

	URGENT	NOT URGENT
IMPORTANT	Quadrant 1 Important and urgent Crises Deadlines Problems	Quadrant 2 Important but not urgent Relationships Planning Recreation
NOT IMPORTANT	Quadrant 3 Not important but urgent Interruptions Meetings Activities	Quadrant 4 Not important and not urgent Time-wasters Pleasant activities Trivia

It's the items in Quadrant 2 that represent the 20% of the things that will bring you 80% of your success.

How amazing would it be if you could reach 80% of your goals by doing 20% of the work?

Hone in on these activities. Put them first. Yes, that does mean you will have to ignore other items. Some of them are easy to ignore, and ideally if you could cut out Quadrants 3 and 4 entirely that would help you massively. In reality though, that's unlikely to happen.

But you can sequence it such that you do Quadrant 2 activities first.

You won't complete a Quadrant 2 activity in a single sitting, but that's not the aim here. The aim is to continually progress on your Quadrant 2 activities. The reason that most of us don't progress has less to do with effort, but more to do with consistency – just spending half an hour a day on your Quadrant 2 activities will get you significantly closer to you goals. In fact, these probably represent 20% of your total activities, which will get you 80% towards the lifestyle you're looking to achieve.

Obviously Quadrant 1 activities need to be done too; they can't really be avoided. But do them as quickly and efficiently as you can, and crucially schedule them after you've done a good shift on your Quadrant 2 activities.

Farhan Qureshi

Chapter 31: Discernment and when to say 'No'

There are two schools of thought on the merits of saying 'No'. One says to always be helpful and to go out of your way to assist other people wherever you can. The other school of thought tells us to, 'Look after number one' i.e. always look for out yourself and never help others unless it's in your own interest.

Clearly the first school of thought has more going for it than the second, but there are a lot of people who nevertheless plump for the second option. It's this second option that tells people how to get to the top, how to be ruthless and step over anyone to achieve what you want. Whilst this may have worked in the '80s and '90s, a lot of people still think this mentality works today. Yet this mindset actually only succeeds to a limited degree and because of the increased transparency that we as a society enjoy, will only get a person so far.

The first option is far preferable, as helping others in itself is very rewarding. You will soon be known as the type of person who goes out of their way to help others – and of course, building up a good reputation will serve you when you need help yourself. However, there will be people who will take advantage of your good nature. You will know who those people are.

You need to be discerning in saying 'No' to requests.

The truth is that you are always saying 'No' to something

'Opportunity cost' is the idea that taking Opportunity A will mean you won't be able to pursue Opportunity B. So therefore the cost of working on Opportunity A is missing out on the benefit of Opportunity B. In effect, you're saying 'No' to one of them.

There's a tendency to think that saying 'No' to someone's request is rude, and nobody wants to appear to be obtuse and unhelpful.

But being able to say 'No' can actually be more helpful to the other person than you half-heartedly agreeing to help them. If you don't have the bandwidth to support the request, then you're better off telling that person (politely, of course) that you're not able to help in this task. This way you don't waste the other person's time and you allow them to pursue other avenues.

It's no longer considered rude to say 'No'. Make it clear that you'd like to help and support them, but you won't be able to on this occasion. Don't give them false hope that you could help on this task in the future; if you can't help, then let them know. Wish them all the best and then move on.

> By actually saying 'Yes' to what you want, you will become successful in your own right. Then you will be in a far better position to help others.

Farhan Qureshi

Chapter 32: Accept your weaknesses, focus on your strengths

Any of us who grew up in the '80s or '90s were most likely exposed to the same philosophy that in order to improve, we must work on our weaknesses. We'd be encouraged (or forced) to spend lots of time and energy working on our weaknesses. Unfortunately this didn't have much effect and by the end of a given period, we would simply be slightly less bad at our weaknesses.

When I think of the amount of time I personally spent working on my weaknesses, I wonder if that time, energy and focus could have been better spent on things that I was actually good at. For example, one of the subjects I took at A-Level was French. It didn't come naturally to me. I spent around 80% of my study time struggling with French – weekends and evenings spent trying to memorise verb conjugation and slowly wading my way through French literature, which I didn't understand. At the end of all this hard toil I managed to get a D grade. The irony is that I got a B grade in Maths, on which I spent a fraction of my time and energy. Had I shifted my focus, even by 10%, I might have got an A in Maths and still attained a D in French.

Fortunately, shifts in educational thinking mean that those growing up today can focus more time and energy on their strengths, rather than trying to be less bad at something that they're not naturally in tune with.

So how can you use this in your day-to-day activities?

Go back and look at your Quadrant 2 activities (Chapters 12 and 30). Given that you filled these in yourself, they most likely will be things that you actually enjoy doing. Because of this, you're quite likely to be good at them.

Now look at the tasks in Quadrant 1, the things that you need to do. Do these tasks play to your natural strengths? Perhaps not. Using the concept of 'interdependence', where we build teams that can work together to achieve more than we could on our own, we can use the collective skills of the team (or outsource) to play to each person's strengths and interests. It's at this intersection of strengths and interest where you will start to achieve your best results and have more fun in doing so.

When you are happy and enjoying what you are doing, you will achieve the success and happiness for which you are searching.

I'm not advocating that you completely abandon those tasks that you're not good at, but just that you try to manage your weaknesses. Figure out the minimum level of attainment you need to reach on your weaker areas and then plug any gaps that exist. Don't spend too long on this; the idea is that when you hit that minimum required level you will then be able to concentrate on your strengths and the things you actually want to do.

Doesn't it sound good to spend more time enjoying what you actually want to do, rather than struggling to be good at something that you don't even want to do?

Farhan Qureshi

Chapter 33: Always continue to move forwards

We've now finished our journey together through this book. I hope it's brought you a lot of value and that you will be able to put these techniques to actionable use.

You now have all the things you need in order to achieve your dreams and make the life for yourself that you've always wanted. Now that you are moving ahead, keep on going. Sometimes it will be easy, sometimes difficult. When you scale one mountain, don't forget to stop to enJoy it.

Remember too that that's not the end of the journey. Go for the next mountain, stopping along the route and enjoy the view as you do so.

It's this continually moving forwards that will build unstoppable momentum, to such an extent where it doesn't feel like you're doing any work, but instead you're spending your days doing what you want and having fun.

Remember to take time out to help others to achieve their goals. Helping others creates a positive aura around yourself. Become a giver without expecting anything in return. By helping others, you are in reality helping yourself, and therefore becoming a receiver – be open to that.

Be patient with other people; everyone is on their own journey and at a different stage on the path. Look at yourself a year ago and think how far you've come. Imagine how much further you'll be a week from now, a month from now and a year from now.

Don't underestimate the effect your smile could have on another person. When you smile at someone, that person will return the smile. What you've done in a small gesture is to change their physiology. They've now smiled and put themselves in a better state of mind. You might have changed their day or even their life for the better.

Always treat yourself with the respect you deserve, regardless of how others treat you. Don't ever look for revenge or to prove other people wrong; you're living your life for yourself, not to gain anybody's recognition.

Finally, you have everything you need; it's already within you. You decide how far you want to go in life. All good things are waiting to come to you – allow yourself to receive them.

Be happy, be kind and enjoy your journey. Don't stress over the outcomes, but instead control the input. Do your best, relax and enjoy life.

Ciao Ciao

If you've read this whole book, well done to you. Thanks for taking the time. As we spoke about right at the start, you have been on a journey and hopefully now know your true self better, the real you that was always there. I hope that through this journey you are able to connect to your higher self and find your unique path, uninhibited from the pressures and expectations of the world around you. Hopefully this book has helped you learn about yourself and will improve the quality of all aspects of your life, from health, to relationships, to have financial freedom and be released of all worries.

If you feel the book has helped you in any way, please leave a positive review on Amazon. If you're reading on Kindle, swiping to the end will prompt you for a review.

I really value your positive reviews as it will help others who are looking for help too. Don't forget to also use your social media platforms to link to the book's Amazon page.

Now that this book has closed, another will open.

The first page of the next book is blank – it's up to you to write it.

Wishing you love, happiness and good health.

Farhan

Come and visit me at my parenting blog www.workingparent.info, at my film and animation blog www.digitopiafilm.com and at my digital blog www.digitopiadigital.com.

Finally, if you are partial to Twitter, I have two handles @farhanq_uk (for my latest creative projects) and @parentworking (for my misadventures in parenting). It will be my pleasure to connect with you there.

www.ingramcontent.com/pod-product-compliance
Lightning Source LLC
Chambersburg PA
CBHW050016090426
42734CB00021B/3286